Computer Oper

The UC

Robin Hunter

Pitman

Computer Handbooks

The complete list of titles in this series and the Pitman Pocket Guide series appears after the Index at the end of this Handbook. The Publishers would welcome suggestions for further additions and improvements to the series.

Consultant Editor: David Hatter

PITMAN PUBLISHING LIMITED
128 Long Acre, London WC2E 9AN

A Longman Group Company

© Robin Hunter 1985
UCSD and UCSD Pascal are registered trademarks of the Regents of the University of California

First edition 1985

British Library Cataloguing in Publication Data

Hunter, Robin, *1938*–
  UCSD p-system — (Computer handbooks)
  1. UCSD p-system (Computer operating system)
  I. Title II. Series
  005.4′46   QA76.6

ISBN 0 273 02196 6

All rights reserved.

Printed in Great Britain at the Bath Press, Avon

Contents

How to Use this Handbook   1
Introduction   2
The Filer   32
The Editor   63
Utilities   84
Appendix   101
Index   104

How to Use this Handbook

This Handbook describes the UCSD Operating System and how to use it. It is mainly intended as a reference book and should be useful to the new, and the more experienced, user of the system. There are four main sections:

Introduction
Filer
Editor
Utilities

In each of the first three sections a short introduction is followed by a description of the relevant system commands arranged in alphabetical order. The purpose of each command is briefly described, followed by an outline of the dialogue to be expected on selecting that command. This is followed in turn by some notes indicating the variety of ways in which the command can be used and also its limitations. Where appropriate, examples of the command being used are also given.

The section on utilities describes some of the system functions used less frequently.

The UCSD system varies little from one implementation to another and beginners who have access to a suitable implementation are encouraged to experiment with it. Once the basic principles of the system have been understood, it is fairly easy to pick up, and hopefully this Handbook will help to smooth over any little difficulties that might arise.

Introduction

The UCSD p-system is an interactive programming environment providing a set of integrated tools for writing and running programs. At the heart of the system is P-code or Pseudo-code, a low-level stack-based language in which the system is written and into which most programs using it are compiled. UCSD P-code, as it is more properly called, is a variation of the P-code designed by Urs Ammann of the Eidgenossische Technische Hochschule in Zurich for implementing Pascal. It is designed to produce compact code which is usually interpreted. The UCSD system itself was designed and implemented originally by Professor Kenneth Bowles and colleagues in the University of California at San Diego and is now maintained by Pecan Software Systems of Brooklyn, New York.

The system is now available on a wide range of personal computers such as the IBM PC, TI Professional, Sirius I, Apple II etc. It is almost identical on the various machines except that the special keys (see p. 6) differ somewhat from machine to machine. The system has developed through a number of versions and here we will describe version IV.13 which is now widely used. It does not vary greatly from versions IV.0 and IV.1. Although designed originally for Pascal, the system now supports FORTRAN, BASIC and a number of other languages. Here we will describe it as if the programming language were Pascal. The dialect of Pascal available under the system is known as UCSD Pascal and differs in a number of ways from the Pascal standard.

Configuration

The personal computer on which you will be running the UCSD system will probably have at least the following configuration:

keyboard
display
central processing unit with at least 64K of main memory
2 disk drives

A printer is another useful peripheral. In addition, there may be extra disk drives or even a hard disk.

Starting up

The process for starting up the UCSD system will vary from one machine to another. It may consist simply of putting a system disk in one disk drive and switching on the power. In some machines, however, it may be important that these two operations are performed in the *opposite* order. The manufacturer's manual should be consulted.

Depending on what checks etc. are performed, it may take several minutes before anything appears on the display screen. Eventually something like the following should appear on the top line of the screen:

Command:E(dit,R(un,F(ile,C(omp,L(ink,X(ecute, A(ssem,D(ebug?[IV.13]

indicating that any of the commands from Edit to Debug can be selected by typing its initial letter (in upper or lower case). This is known as the main menu. There are some more options available from the main menu as can be seen by typing '?'.

Command:H(alt,I(nitialize,U(ser restart, M(onitor[IV.13]

Whichever of the two lines of commands is visible, any of the options may be selected. In addition to the main menu, a manufacturer's logo may fill the rest of the screen when the system is started up.

Menus

Menus, like the main menu illustrated above, are a feature of the UCSD system. As a general rule a menu offers a number of options, any one of which may be selected by typing its initial letter in either upper or lower case without a following <ret>(return). Selecting some options will lead to further menus which can be selected from in a similar way. The full hierarchy of commands is illustrated in Figure 1. Notice the tree structure. Selecting from a menu takes you one level 'down' the tree. To come back up a level, Q for Quit can normally be typed.

In some cases, selecting a command will lead to a question, the answer to which is a string, for example the name of a file. In this case the name of the file or whatever should be typed *followed by* <ret>. As was illustrated with the main menu, not all the options of a particular menu may appear on the screen at the one time. In fact, some little-used options may never appear on the screen but are none the less available whatever selection of options

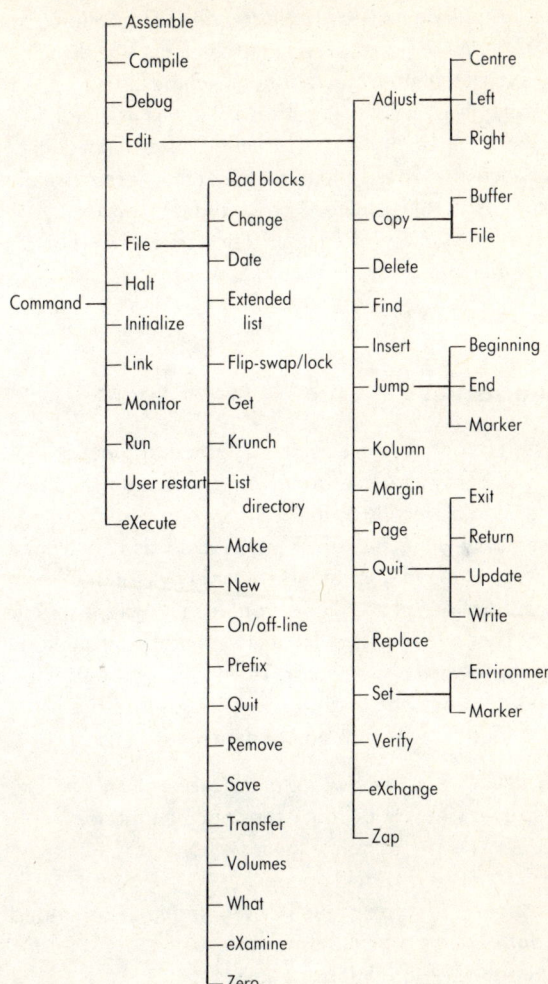

Figure 1

is currently being shown. Nearly all of the options for each menu are discussed in detail in this Handbook.

Two of the main menu options will be chosen frequently by most users. These are the File and Edit options which allow access to the filer and the editor respectively. These two modules of the system are of particular significance to programmers, and much of this Handbook is taken up in detailed explanation of how they are used.

Special keys

A number of keys are used for particular functions in the UCSD system and are given special names. Some are used generally by the system while others are used only within the editor. As keyboards vary from one machine to another, the actual keys (or combinations of keys) used for these functions varies too. The following is a list of the special key functions and what they are used for. The names of the special keys are enclosed in angle brackets as they are throughout the Handbook and on menus etc.

<ret>	to produce a carriage return
<space>	to produce the space character
<bs>	to delete the last character (backspace)
<esc>	to escape from (or leave) a command
<del>	to delete the current line
<break>	to interrupt a program
<stop/start>	to stop/start a program temporarily
<flush>	to suppress output to the console

<eof>	to produce an end of file from the keyboard

Editor keys

<tab>	to move the cursor to the next tab stop
<up>	to move the cursor up one line
<down>	to move the cursor down one line
<left>	to move the cursor one place to the left
<right>	to move the cursor one place to the right
<exch-ins>	to insert a character within eXchange
<exch-del>	to delete a character within eXchange
<etx>	to accept an insertion or deletion

To illustrate the actual keys that might be used for these functions, the keys used in one implementation, the IBM PC, are now listed:

	IBM PC
<ret>	↵
<space>	space
<bs>	←
<esc>	esc
<del>	ctrl+bs
<break>	ctrl+break
<stop/start>	ctrl+s
<flush>	ctrl+f
<eof>	ctrl+c
<tab>	↦
<up>	↑
<down>	↓

<left>	←
<right>	→
<exch-ins>	Ins
<exch-del>	Del
<etx>	ctrl+c

where a notation such as

ctrl+c

means that the control key should be held down while the key for c is depressed.

Use of disks

The computer system used to run the UCSD system will normally have two disk drives. Depending on what the system is being used for, a number of system files will require to be present. One disk drive will normally have the system disk from which the system is booted permanently mounted on it. The following files must be on the system disk:

SYSTEM.PASCAL
SYSTEM.MISCINFO
SYSTEM.INTERP

In addition:

SYSTEM.STARTUP
SYSTEM.MENU
SYSTEM.LIBRARY
SYSTEM.WRK.TEXT
SYSTEM.WRK.CODE

if present, must be on the system disk.

In most applications, the following files will also need to be present though not necessarily on the system disk:

SYSTEM.EDITOR
SYSTEM.FILER
SYSTEM.COMPILER
SYSTEM.LINKER

and preferably

SYSTEM.SYNTAX

The manufacturer's manual should explain what the various system files are used for. The user will also want to be able to store his own text and code files on disk and will wish to configure his disks to minimize the frequency with which they have to be changed.

Workfiles

A philosophy of any good operating system is that it should be relatively simple to do simple things. For example, it should not require the full power of the editor and the filer to enter a simple program and to compile and run it. To save the user having to name files at each stage of such a sequence, the idea of a workfile is present in the UCSD system. Two workfiles are made available automatically, called:

SYSTEM.WRK.TEXT
SYSTEM.WRK.CODE

and are the default files used by Compile, Run and Edit, the first being used for the source code and the second for object code. We will refer to these files as the TEXT and CODE workfiles respectively. It is also possible for the TEXT and CODE versions of some other file to be specified as workfiles. The filer has commands which can be used to choose a workfile, store the contents of the workfiles in named files and so on.

The file SYSTEM.LST.TEXT is sometimes also thought of as a workfile. It is used as the default file for compiler listings when the L compiler option is present. For more details, see under Compile.

Workspace

Part of the main memory of the computer is available to the user as workspace for editing files. The normal procedure is that the file to be edited is copied into this workspace and the editing performed on this copy. After editing has been completed, the contents of the workspace can be copied back on to disk either under the old file name or a new name. In particular, the TEXT workfile may be edited and updated in this way without referring to it by name. Part of the main memory is also reserved for the copy buffer (see p.66) and for the scratch input buffers (see under eXecute p.28).

Pascal systems

Two (or possibly more) Pascal systems are normally available, one which uses two-word (32-bit) real numbers and one which uses four-word (64-bit) reals. Object programs with four-word reals will be larger and run slower than those with two-word reals. However, the results will be more accurate with the 4-word real numbers. From version IV.1 of the UCSD system onwards, four-word reals are used by default. To obtain a system using two-word reals, modifications may have to be made to some of the system software. Details of how to make the modifications should be given in the manufacturer's manual.

Separate compilation

A UCSD Pascal program may contain *units* which have been compiled separately and saved in a library. The exact syntax of a unit is not given here but each will consist of two parts: an interface part, the details of which are available to other units or programs using the unit; and an implementation part whose details are not known outside the unit.

A program (or unit) that requires the presence of a precompiled unit should contain a *uses* statement of the form

uses mathfuns

On encountering a *uses* statement, the compiler will expect to find the unit referred to either in the text being compiled or in the file

SYSTEM.LIBRARY

unless the default library file has been changed using a U compiler option (see under Compile) of the form

uses {$U MYLIB.CODE} unita

Alternatively, the file USERLIB.TEXT can be used to store the names of the files to be searched for *use*d units *before* SYSTEM.LIBRARY is searched.

The LIBRARY utility can be used for transferring units from one file to another. The Link command can be used to link native code routines together or to link native code routines into Pascal units or programs.

How to use the various main menu commands is now described. In many cases the reply to a prompt is given as

file-spec

which represents the name of a file, the precise format of which is given in the section on the filer. *volume-id* is also defined in the filer section.

Assemble

Use
To assemble programs held as text files

After selecting Assemble, the following will appear:

Assembling . . .

If SYSTEM.WRK.TEXT is on the system disk, the text therein will be assembled. Otherwise, if another file has been named as a workfile, the .TEXT version of that file will be assembled. If there is no text workfile, the following prompt will appear:

Prompt	*Reply*
Assemble what text?	*file-spec*

where *file-spec* denotes the file whose text is to be assembled. It should not include the suffix .TEXT as this will be added automatically.

If SYSTEM.WRK.TEXT or a named workfile is being assembled, the resultant code will be written to SYSTEM.WRK.CODE. If a file other than a workfile is being assembled, the name of a code file will then be requested:

To what code-file?   *file-spec*

where *file-spec* denotes the file in which the object code should be stored. It should not include the suffix .CODE as this will be added automatically. A reply of '$' will denote a code file with the same name as the text file but with the suffix .CODE in place of .TEXT. This file will be on the *default volume* unless the '$' is preceded by a *volume-id*. A reply of <ret> will cause SYSTEM.WRK.CODE to be used as the code file.

In a short time the following prompt should appear:

Output file for assembled listing(<cr> for none)

the reply to which should specify a text file or perhaps PRINTER: or CONSOLE:, or <ret> for no listing.

If an error is found during assembly, the prompt

Type <sp> to continue,<esc> to terminate, or 'e' to edit

appears. <esc> aborts,<space> allows assembly to continue while 'e' enters the editor with the cursor showing the place in the source file where the error was discovered.

When Assembly is complete, the code file produced is normally linked into a Pascal program to be executed. Assembly requires the presence of the file SYSTEM.ASSMBLER and opcode and error files which will not necessarily be present in a Pascal environment.

Compile

Use
To compile programs held as text files.

After selecting Compile, the following will appear:

Compiling . . .

If SYSTEM.WRK.TEXT is on the system disk, the text therein will be compiled. Otherwise, if another file has been named as the workfile, the contents of the .TEXT version of this file will be compiled. If there is no TEXT workfile, the following prompt will appear:

Prompt	*Reply*
Compile what text?	file-spec

where *file-spec* denotes the file whose text is to be compiled. It should not include the suffix .TEXT as this will be added automatically.

If SYSTEM.WRK.TEXT or a named workfile is being compiled, the resultant code will be written to SYSTEM.WRK.CODE. If a file other than a workfile is being compiled, the name of a code file will be requested.

To what code-file?   *file-spec*

where *file-spec* denotes the file in which the object code should be stored. It should not include the suffix .CODE as this will be added automatically. A reply of $ will denote a code file with the same name as the text file but with the suffix .CODE in place of .TEXT. This file will be on the *default volume* unless the '$' is preceded by a *volume-id*. A reply of <ret> will cause SYSTEM.WRK.CODE to be used as the code file.

In a short time the following prompt should appear:

Output file for compiled listing?(<cr> for none)

the reply to which should specify a text file or perhaps PRINTER: or CONSOLE:, or <ret> for no listing.

The compiler will then begin compiling the text of the program and something like the following should appear during the first pass of the compiler, assuming for the moment that no errors are found in the program:

Pascal compiler – release level IV.13c6t-4
<   0>.....
READIN
<   5>......
MIN
< 11>......
COMPLIST
< 17>..
COMPLIST...

The numbers in the angle brackets above denote the number of lines compiled so far and each dot represents a line compiled. The name of each function or procedure encountered is also printed.

If the compiler discovers an error in the program, two lines or so of it including the point where the error was discovered, will be printed, for example:

end;
function min(q:array10); <—

followed by something like

Error #123
Line 9
Type <sp> to continue,<esc> to terminate, or 'e' to edit

allowing the user to continue compilation, abandon compilation or return to the editor to amend the source file. If the latter option is chosen, part of the TEXT workfile (if this is what was being compiled) will be displayed with the cursor indicating at which point in the text the error was discoverd. This, of course, is not necessarily where the programming error was made. An error message may also be displayed at this stage. A prompt will indicate that the editor may be invoked by pressing space.

If a file other than the TEXT workfile was being compiled before the edit option was chosen, the following prompt will appear:

No workfile is present. File? (<ret> for no file)

allowing the user to specify the file to be edited.

If CONSOLE: is specified for the compiled listing and no syntax errors are discovered by the first pass of the compiler, the second pass will display the following (or something similar):

Pascal Compiler IV.13 c6t-4 12/17/84

Page 1

```
 1  2  1:d   1   program complist(input,output);
 2  2  1:d   1   type array10 = array[1..10] of
                      integer;
 3  2  1:d   1   var b:array10;
 4  2  1:d  11   procedure readin(var a:array10);
 5  2  2:d   1   var i:1..10;
 6  2  2:0   0   begin for i := 1 to 10 do
 7  2  2:2  15        read(a[i])
 8  2  1:0   0   end;
 9  2  1:d   1   function min(a:array10):integer;
10  2  3:d   1   var i:2..10;
11  2  3:d   2       small:integer;
12  2  3:0   5   begin small := a[1];
13  2  3:1  15        for i := 2 to 10 do
14  2  3:2  30           if a[i] <small
15  2  3:2  39           then small := a[i];
16  2  3:1  58        min :=small
17  2  1:0   0   end;
18  2  1:0   0   begin readin(b);
19  2  1:1   4         writeln(min(b))
20  2   :0   0   end.
```
End of compilation

Each line of the compilation listing is of the form

<line number><segment number>
<routine number>:<nesting depth><space><text>

For a line containing a declaration, the *nesting depth* is given as 'd'. The *space* field of each line is the amount of code or data space required by the routine at that point.

Compiler options
A compiler option may appear in a Pascal program to indicate to the compiler how the compilation should be performed, whether the source code should be listed etc. A compiler option takes the form of a Pascal comment whose first character is a '$'. This is followed by the initial letter of the option name, followed by a parameter in most cases. Some options take the parameter + or − which has the effect of switching the option on (+) or off (−). Each of these options has a default setting and in some cases values of these options may be stacked to a depth of 15. When a new value is given to such an option, the old value is stacked and when ^ is used as the parameter of such an option the value is taken from the stack. The 'stack' options are I/O check, Range-check and the conditional compilation options (Declare, Begin and End). For details, see below.

Other options have a string parameter usually denoting a file name. For example:

{$I NEWPROC}

will use the INCLUDE option to switch the compiler input to come from the file called NEWPROC. A number of compiler options may be grouped, for example:

{$R+,I NEWPROC}

in which case only the last option may have a string parameter.

The following are some of the options normally available:

BEGIN(B)
: marks the start of a section of code to be conditionally compiled depending on the value of a flag

COPYRIGHT(C)
: allows a string to be placed in the copyright field of the code file

DECLARE(D)
: sets a flag to be used in connection with conditional compilation

END(E)
: marks the end of a section of code to be conditionally compiled

INCLUDE(I)
: switches compiler input to named file at end of which input reverts to original file

I/O CHECK(I)
: allows the compiler to stop generating test code after every I/O statement by specifying I− (default I+)

LIST(L)
: produces a listing of the program on the root volume in a file called SYSTEM.LST.TEXT when switched on (L+) or in any file or on a character device if L is followed by a *file-spec*, e.g. {$L PRINTER:} (default L−)

PAGE(P)	produces a new page when a listing is being printed, i.e. {$P} produces a new page. {$P+} (the default) produces pages 8½ inches long. {$P−} produces no automatic pagination
QUIET(Q)	suppresses most of the screen display apart from error reporting when Q+ is specified (default Q− for most terminals)
RANGE CHECK(R)	includes range checks in the object code by specifying R+ (default R+)
USER(U)	allows the program to use unit names belonging to the operating system by specifying U− before program or unit appears (default U+)
USES(U)	provides access to UNITs when separate compilation is involved by specifying a code file where they may be found

Conditional compilation

The DECLARE option can be used to set a flag, for example:

{$D SWITCH+}

in which the + indicates that any piece of program which follows and is surrounded by

{$B SWITCH}

and

{$E SWITCH}

should be compiled. Similarly, a − in the declare option would inhibit the compilation of such a piece of program.

DECLARE is a stack option and each flag must be introduced by means of a DECLARE option before the initial reserved word *program* or *unit*. Subsequent occurrences of the DECLARE option may switch the flag on (+) or off (−).

Debug

Use
To find errors in programs.

The debugger can be used to set break points in programs, examine the values of variables, single step through P-code etc. Use of the debugger involves an understanding of the internal details of the P-system beyond the scope of this text.

Edit

Use
To alter an existing text file or create a new one.

On selecting Edit if no TEXT workfile is present, the following prompt appears:

>Edit:
No Workfile is present. File?(<ret> for no file)

If the user types <ret>, the editor assumes that a new TEXT workfile is to be created and the editor menu will appear

>Edit: A(djust C(opy D(el F(ind I(nsert J(ump K(ol M(argin P(age?[IV.1F7b]

The new file is initially empty and text can be inserted in it using Insert. If the user wishes to edit an existing file he should reply to the prompt

>Edit:
No workfile is present. File?(<ret>for no file)

with a file specification (*file-spec*). Note that in this instance the *file-spec* should *not* contain the suffix .TEXT as this will be added automatically by the editor.

The third possibility is that a TEXT workfile is present when the editor is entered, in which case this text file will be copied into the workspace and displayed on the screen ready for editing.

Editor commands
The various editor commands are described in detail in the section on the editor (p.00).

Leaving the editor
To leave the editor, the user should select Quit from the menu when the following options will be given:

>Quit:
    U(pdate the workfile and leave
    E(xit without updating
    R(eturn to the editor without updating
    W(rite to a file name and return

When a workfile is being used, Update will be the normal reply. This will copy the text in the workspace into the file SYSTEM.WRK.TEXT and *then* remove any previous version of this file. If any problem arises in copying the contents of the workspace on to disk, the previous version of the workfile will still be present. This means that there must be space on the disk concerned for both the old and the new versions of the workfile and one of the problems that can arise is that there is insufficient space for *both* copies. If necessary the Write option can be used to save the file on another disk (make sure you always have a spare disk ready initialized!). When Update has been successfully executed, the message

Your file is *n* bytes long

where *n* is an integer, is displayed, the system leaves the editor and the main menu appears again.

Selecting Exit also leaves the editor but without saving the contents of the workspace on disk.

Selecting Return takes you back to the editor, reinstating the situation before Quit was selected — useful if you did not mean to leave the editor in the first place.

Selecting Write if the contents of the workspace were not copied from a disk file in the first place leads to the following prompt:

Prompt	*Reply*
Quit:	
Name of output file (<cr> to return)—>	*file-spec*

Again the suffix .TEXT will be added to *file-spec* automatically and should not be included. *file-spec* gives the name of the file into which the contents of the workspace should be copied. Typing <ret> to the above prompt returns to the editor without copying the contents of the workspace.

If the contents of the workspace were originally copied from a permanent disk file (possibly the workfile), the following prompt will appear:

Quit:
$<ret> writes to *file-spec*
Name of output file(<cr> to return) —>

where *file-spec* refers to the file from which the contents of the workspace were originally copied. A reply of '$' followed by <ret> will copy the text in the workspace back into this file and remove the old version. Alternatively the reply may be a *file-spec* denoting some other file into which the contents of the workspace should be copied. Again, if the reply is simply <ret> the system will return to the editor without copying the contents of the workspace on to disk.

If no problems arise, the following message should appear on writing the contents of the workspace to disk:

>Quit:
Writing. .
Your file is *n* bytes long
Do you want to E(xit or R(eturn to the editor?

A reply of Exit will leave the editor as described earlier. A reply of Return will return to the editor and reinstate the situation before Quit was selected. It is often useful for safety reasons to copy a partially edited file to disk and then return to the editor.

File

Use
To manage the file system.

On selecting File, the filer menu appears:

Filer:G(et,S(ave,W(hat,N(ew,L(dir,R(em,C(hng,
T(rans,D(ate?[D.9]

showing some of the options available. Other options can be seen by typing '?' Any option can be selected by typing its initial letter whether or not it is currently shown on the menu.

Filer commands
The various filer commands are described in detail in the section on the filer (p.32).

Leaving the filer
Q (for Quit) is typed to leave the filer whereupon the main menu will reappear:

Halt

Use
To stop execution of the p-system.

The system must be rebooted to start it again after this command (some systems may reboot automatically).

Initialize

Use
To initialize the p-system.

Initialize brings the system back to a standard state rebuilding the system's internal tables, etc.

Link

Use
To link program segments together where this is not done automatically.

Selecting Link causes the program in the file SYSTEM.LINKER to be executed giving the prompt

Host file?

the reply to which should be a file name to which .CODE is added automatically unless the name ends in '.'. A reply of <ret> leads to the CODE workfile being used as the host file. The host file will usually contain a program into which separately compiled units or (more often) assembly code routines have to be linked. Once the name of the host file has been supplied, the next prompt is

Lib file?

the reply to which is the file containing the first unit or routine to be linked in. This prompt will be displayed repeatedly until a reply of <ret> indicates that there are no more units or routines to be linked in. The prompt

Map name?

then appears. If a text file is supplied as a response, the details of the linkage will be entered there. A reply of <ret> means that linkage details are not stored. The prompt

Output file?

then appears requesting the name of a file in which to store the linked code. This may be the original host file. A reply of <ret> will imply that the CODE workfile is to be used. Linking will then take place and, if successful, the program in the output file may then be eXecuted.

Monitor

Use
To set up a command file to be used as system input.

On selecting Monitor, the following prompt line appears:

Monitor:B(egin, E(nd, A(bort, S(uspend, R(esume

To set up a command file to be used as a script for system input, Begin should first be selected. A prompt

Write to what file?

then asks for the name of a file in which to store subsequent user commands. When this has been supplied, Resume should then be selected to return to the main menu. Thereafter all user input will be recorded in the file named until Monitor is again selected followed by End and Resume to return to the main menu. The Suspend option (within Monitor) may be used to stop recording user commands temporarily until Resume (within Monitor) is selected. Abort causes the command file to be scrapped.

An Execution option (see under eXecute) can be used to redirect system input to be taken from the command file.

Run

Use
To compile (if necessary) and execute the text or code in the current workfile.

Run will compile the TEXT workfile if it has been edited since it was last compiled or there is no CODE workfile. It will then execute the corresponding code file. Otherwise it will simply execute the CODE workfile.

User restart

Use
To rerun a program.

eXecute

Use
To execute a compiled program.

Prompt	Reply
Execute what file?	*execution-option-string*

where *execution-option-string* may simply name a code file (without the .CODE suffix) to be executed. However, it may also contain *option specifications* or may contain only option specifications. The name of the code file (if present) will precede any option specifications but they will be implemented *before* the code file is executed.

The following option specifications are available:

I	redirects system input
L	changes the default library
O	redirects system output
P	changes the prefix (default) volume
PI	redirects program input
PO	redirects program output

For example, the execution option string

HANOI P=TESTS L=NEWLIB I=MON

will change the default prefix to

TESTS:

then it will change the default library to the text file

TESTS:NEWLIB.TEXT

then it will change the system input to be taken from

TESTS:MON

and finally the file

TESTS:HANOI.CODE

will be executed. Notice that the suffices .TEXT and

.CODE are added to the library and code files respectively. The various options will be implemented in the following order:

(1) new default prefix
(2) new default library
(3) I/O redirections (in any order)
(4) execution of the file (if specified)

Redirecting the system input to be taken from a text file amounts to driving the system from a predetermined script. Such a script can be set up using Monitor.

Redirection options
The system and program inputs may be taken from a file (or a character device) or from a *scratch input buffer*. Two character buffers are available in the main memory as scratch input buffers, one for storing system input and one for program input. If the parameter following the equals sign in an I or PI option is a string (delimited by double quotes), the input will be taken from the appropriate scratch input buffer and the string itself will be added to the end of the buffer, the buffer thus being used in a first-in first-out manner. As a special (but commonly occurring) case, if the buffer is empty when the I or PI option is implemented the string itself will be the input to the system or program. Within this string a carriage return will be represented by a comma and a double quote by a pair of double quotes. For example, if the system scratch input buffer was initially empty,

Execute what file?I="fd1–J–86,q"

would cause the filer to be entered, the date altered, then a return to the main menu.

The parameter on the right-hand side of the equals sign in any of the redirection options may be empty, with the following effects:

I=   (O=)

resets the system input (output) to CONSOLE: (i.e. ends the redirection) whereas

PI=   (PO=)

resets the program input (output) to be the same as the system input (output).

System redirection will continue (in the absence of another redirection command) until Halt is selected or a runtime error occurs. The Initialize command will *not* affect any system redirection in force though it will cause the contents of the system scratch input buffer to be lost. Program redirection will terminate when the program terminates, at which stage the contents of the program scratch input buffer are lost.

The Filer

The filer is the operating system module responsible for looking after user (and other) files and communicating with external devices. The filer menu is

Filer:G(et,S(ave,W(hat,N(ew,L(dir,R(em,C(hng, T(rans,D(ate? [D.9]

the question mark indicating that further options can be obtained by typing '?'. These are:

Filer:Q(uit,B(ad-blks,E(xt-dir,K(rnch,M(ake,P(refix, V(ols? [D.9]

and

Filer:X(amine,Z(ero,O(n/off-line,F(lip-swap/lock [D.9]

Each of these commands is discussed in detail later in this section. First we have to define a few terms.

File-name

A file-name may consist of up to 15 characters including

letters A–Z
digits 0–9
period, underline, dash, slash and backslash

A file-name may include a suffix indicating its type, for example:

.TEXT   text file (for programs)
.BACK   backup text file

.CODE   code file
.BAD   file containing bad blocks
.SVOL   subsidiary volume file

Where *file-name* appears in italics in this section it stands for any file-name as defined above.

File specification

In many situations a file-name is not sufficient to specify a file. A file specification will also include information about where the file may be found. A file may reside on a storage volume (e.g. a disk) or may correspond to an input or output device (referred to as a communications volume). Storage volumes may be referred to by a name or by the device number of the device on which they are mounted. Communication volumes have standard names and device numbers, see below.

A file specification is then of the form

volume-id file-name

where *volume-id* is one of

: (or blank)   meaning the default volume
*   meaning the system volume
              (from which the system was booted)
volume-name: i.e. a named volume
device number: i.e. a volume mounted on a specific device

A *device number* is of the form

#m

where m is a positive integer. A *volume-id* may consist of a device number (without the following ':') if it is *not* followed by a file-name.

A volume-name is defined similarly to a file-name but may not have more than seven characters.

The standard device numbers and their volume-names are:

Device No.	Volume name	Meaning
#1	CONSOLE	Keyboard and display
#2	SYSTERM	Keyboard and display (no echo)
#4		First disk drive (system disk)
#5		Second disk drive
#6	PRINTER	Printer
#7	REMIN	Serial input
#8	REMOUT	Serial output

Examples of valid *volume-ids* are:

PRINTER:	(Printer device)
#4:	(First disk drive)
#1:	(Console)
:	(Default volume)
*	(System volume)
PASCAL:	(Disk with volume name 'PASCAL')

Where *volume-name* (or *volume-id*) appears in italics in this section, it stands for any volume name (or volume-id) as defined above.

Examples of valid file specifications are:

SYSTEM4:SYSTEM.EDITOR
PASCAL:SHELLSORT.TEXT
#4:SYSTEM.WRK.TEXT
*SYSTEM.PASCAL

:MAZE.CODE
MAZE.CODE (same as :MAZE.CODE)

Where *file-spec* appears in italics in this section, it stands for any file-specification as defined above.

Size specification

When a file is created, a file specification followed by a size specification is required. This is referred to as a *size-spec* and is either

[*]
[0]
[positive integer]

For details of how *size-specs* are used, see under the command Make.

Wild cards

There are three wild card characters which can be used to avoid typing the same or a similar file specification a number of times. These are:

$
=
?

$ means 'the same file-name as before' and can be used for example in Transfer to copy a file from one volume to another without changing its name.

If we want to specify a set of files with similar names, = can be used to stand for any sequence of characters in a file name so that

=.TEXT

would stand for the set of all file names ending in
.TEXT and a valid file specification (in certain
contexts) would be

#4:=.TEXT

implying that the current operation should be
applied to all the files on the volume on drive 4
ending in .TEXT.

The ? wild card is used in a similar way to = except
that the user will be prompted to type 'y' or 'n' for
each file in the set to determine whether the current
operation should be applied to it or not.

The following filer commands may use wild cards:

Change	On/off line
Extended list	Remove
List directory	Transfer

Only one wild card character may appear in a file
specification.

File types

File names ending in .TEXT or .BACK (for a backup
file) are used to hold text such as programs etc. They
have a special format including a two-block header
page which is held on disk but is not transferred to
an output device when the file is printed. Some
commands require you to supply a file-name ending
in .TEXT, others add it automatically in which case
the suffix .TEXT should *not* be included. However, if,
for some reason, you do wish to supply the .TEXT
suffix in these cases, an extra period following the
suffix will prevent the .TEXT being added by any of
the commands.

File names ending in .CODE contain compiled programs. They also have a special format. As for text files, some commands expect you to supply a .CODE file, others add the .CODE for you and an extra period at the end of a file name will prevent the suffix being added.

File names ending in .BAD are used to cover damaged blocks on a disk.

File names ending in .SVOL are used for subsidiary volumes, a facility available from version IV.1 of the UCSD system onwards. A subsidiary volume is a disk file which behaves like a storage volume in its own right, having its own files and directory. In this way we can have a hierarchy of files and are not restricted to having at most 77 files on a disk as would otherwise be the case. However, a subsidiary volume may not have a file which is itself a subsidiary volume.

A subsidiary volume may be set up using the Make command in the filer and supplying a file name which includes the suffix .SVOL. A subsidiary volume must contain at least 11 blocks and may have a duplicate directory. On/off line may be used to mount or dismount a subsidiary volume. The command Volumes will display the names of all volumes (including subsidiary volumes) which are on-line.

Bad blocks

Use
To search a disk for faulty blocks:

Prompt	*Reply*
Bad block scan of what vol?	volume-id
Scan for *m* blocks?(Y/N)	y/n *
Scan for how many blocks?	p **

where *m* and *p* are integers and *m* is the number of blocks on the volume.

  * appears if the volume has a valid directory.

  ** appears if you don't want to scan the entire volume for bad blocks

Notes

(1) If 'bad' blocks are found, a message such as the following may appear:

  Block 20 is bad
  Block 21 is bad
  2 bad blocks
  File(s) endangered
  PROG.CODE 20 29

  blocks 20–29 being the location of PROG.CODE.
  If no bad blocks are found the message

  0 bad blocks

  should appear.

(2) It may be possible to 'fix' bad blocks using eXamine (see later).

Example

Bad block scan of what vol? PASCAL:
Scan for 320 blocks? y
Block 201 is bad

1 bad block
File(s) endangered;
PROG1.TEXT 200 250

Change

Use
To alter the name of a file or a storage volume.

To alter a file name

Prompt	Reply
Change what file?	*file-spec*
Change to what?	*new-file-name*
Remove old *volume-name:new-file-name?*	y/n *
Volume-name:file-name —> *new-file-name*	

* appears if there is already a file called *new-file-name* on the disk. The last line will appear if you type 'y' or there was no file called *new-file-name* on the disk.

A wild card may be used in *file-spec* above provided the same wild card is used in the corresponding position in *new-file-name*. Each string corresponding to the wild card in *file-spec* will replace the wild card in the corresponding *new-file-name*.

Alternatively

Prompt	Reply
Change what file?	*file-spec, new-file-name*

volume-name:file-name —>
  new-file-name

To alter the name of a volume

Prompt	Reply
Change what file?	*volume-id*
Change to what?	*new-volume-name:*

volume-name: —> *new-volume-name:*

Examples
(1) Change what file? #5:PROG1.TEXT
    Change to what? PROG101.TEXT
    PASCAL:PROG1.TEXT —> PROG101.TEXT
(2) Change what file? MYPROGS:, OLDPROGS:
    MYPROGS:—> OLDPROGS:
(3) Change what file? :NAMES
    Change to what? DATA
    Remove old INFO:DATA? y
    INFO:NAMES —> DATA
(4) Change what file? PROG=,MYPROG=
    DEF:PROG.TEXT —> MYPROG.TEXT
    DEF:PROG.CODE —> MYPROG.CODE

Date

Use
To display or change the date.

Prompt	Reply
Date set:<1. .31>–<Jan. .Dec> –<00. .99>	
Today is *day-month-year*	
New date ?	*day-month-year*
The date is *day-month-year*	

Notes
(1) If only a day or only a day and a month are given, then the other field(s) of date are unchanged.
(2) If the reply is simply return, the date is unchanged.

Examples
(1) Date set: <1. .31>–<Jan. .Dec>–<00. .99>
    Today is 6–Jun–84
    New date ? 7
    The date is 7–Jun–84
(2) date set: <1. .31>–<Jan. .Dec>–<00. .99>
    Today is 6–Jun–84
    New date ? 25–Dec–85
    The date is 25–Dec–85

eXamine

See alphabetically under X

Extended list (Ext-dir on menu)

Use
To give a fuller listing of a directory than given by List. Partial directories or individual directory entries may also be listed.

To list a single entry:

Prompt	Reply
Dir listing of what vol?	file-spec

The reply would have the following form:

41

file-name length date start bytes type

where

date is the date when the file was last modified
start is the block number at which the file starts
bytes is the number of bytes in the last block of the file
type is the type of the file, e.g. Codefile, Datafile, Textfile.

A typical reply might therefore be:

SYSTEM.FILER 32 1–Jan–85 135 512 Codefile

If *file-spec* contained wild cards, a number of entries could be listed. When a listing contains more than one directory entry it is preceded by

volume-name:

on a separate line and followed by a line such as

2/21 files <listed/in-dir>, 300 blocks used, 20 unused, 8 in largest

which is self-explanatory.

To list a complete directory:

Prompt	Reply
Dir listing of what vol?	volume-id

The listing could be sent to a file by using a reply of the form:

volume-id, file-spec

For example, if the *file-spec* is PRINTER: the listing will be on the printer.

Extended list (unlike List) applied to a complete volume will show the positions of unused blocks on a disk.

Examples
(1) Dir listing of what vol? SYSTEM4, PRINTER:
(2) Dir listing of what vol? #4:SYSTEM.PASCAL
    SYSTEM.PASCAL 101 2–Jan–84 6 512
    Datafile
(3) Dir listing of what vol? #5:=.TEXT
    PASCAL:
    BINCHOP.TEXT 22 25–Dec–84 8 512 Textfile
    HANOI.TEXT 10   6–Dec–84 10 512 Textfile
    2/10 files <listed/in-dir>, 100 blocks used, 100 unused, 100 in largest

Flip swap/lock

Use
To allow the complete filer to be resident or non-resident.

The first time that Flip swap/lock is selected, a message such as

Filer segments memlocked. [5088 words]

will appear indicating that all the filer segments will be kept in main memory and that 5088 16-bit words are available as workspace. Selecting F again will cause a message such as

Filer segments swappable.[10135 words]

to appear, indicating that not all the filer segments will be kept in main memory and 10135 words are available for workspace. The filer can operate in two modes: memlocked (all in memory) and memswapped (only part in memory at a time), and selecting F will change from one mode to the other, the initial state being memswapped. When maximum workspace is required, the filer should be memswapped but when it is more important to save time spent swapping filer segments in and out of memory, then the filer should be memlocked.

Get

Use
To designate files as workfiles.

Prompt	Reply
Throw away current workfile?	y/n *
Get what file?	file-spec

*appears if SYSTEM.WRK.TEXT or SYSTEM.WRK.CODE are on the system disk. 'y' will remove them. 'n' will cancel Get. Save can be used to copy existing workfiles. *file-spec* should not include .TEXT or .CODE. If either is present, it is ignored.

The response from the system will depend on whether it is able to find the named files. It will look for:

file-spec.TEXT
file-spec.CODE

and will display:

Text and Code file loaded

if both can be found. If one or other or both of the files cannot be found, then one of the following messages will be displayed as appropriate:

Text file loaded
Code file loaded
No file loaded

Wild cards are not allowed.

Examples
(1) Get what file? #5:LIFEGAME
    Text and Code file loaded
(2) Get what file? PROGS:SORT
    Text file loaded

Krunch

Use
To consolidate unused blocks on a disk.

Prompt	Reply
Crunch what vol?	volume-id
From end of disk, block *m*?(Y/N)	y/n
Starting at block #?	p *
Moving forward *file-name1*	
Moving forward *file-name2*	
.	
.	
Moving backward *file-name n*	
volume-name: crunched	

where *m* and *p* are positive integers.
  * appears if 'n' is given as the reply to the previous prompt. It asks where the crunching should begin.

45

Notes
(1) Files are normally moved forward towards the beginning of the disk. However, if a starting block number is given, files before that block are moved forward, and files after that block are moved backwards towards the end of the disk thus leaving space in the centre. The starting block number must not, of course, lie within a file.
(2) Before 'crunching' a disk it is advisable to use Bad blocks to check for damaged blocks.
(3) If SYSTEM.PASCAL or SYSTEM.FILER are moved by the Krunch operation it will be necessary to re-initialize the system before proceeding.
(4) Subsidiary volumes may be 'Krunched' like any other volume.

Example
Crunch what vol? PROGS:
From end of disk, block 200?(Y/N) n
Starting at block #? 100
Moving forward SEARCH
Moving forward PRICES
Moving backward PRIMES
Moving backward TREE
Moving backward SORT
PROGS: crunched

List directory

Use
To list details of some or all the files in a directory.
(Extended list gives fuller details.)

To list a single entry:

Prompt	Reply
Dir listing of what vol?	*file-spec*

The reply would have the following form:

file-name length date

where *date* is the date when the file was last modified.

A typical reply might therefore be

SYSTEM.FILER 32 1–Jan–85

If *file-spec* contained wild cards, a number of entries could be listed. When a listing contains more than one directory entry it is preceded by

volume-name:

on a separate line and followed by a line such as

4/8 files <listed/in-dir>,210 blocks used, 110 unused, 110 in largest

which is self-explanatory.

To list a complete directory:

Prompt	Reply
Dir listing of what vol?	*volume-id*

The listing could be sent to a file by giving a reply of the form

volume-id, file-spec

For example, if the *file-spec* is PRINTER: the listing will be on the printer.

Examples
(1) Dir listing of what vol? PASCAL:, PRINTER:
(2) Dir listing of what vol? #5:BINCHOP.TEXT
     BINCHOP.TEXT   40   31-Dec-84
(3) Dir listing of what vol? :SYSTEM=
     PBOOT:
     SYSTEM.PASCAL   101   2-Jan-84
     SYSTEM.INTERP   26   2-Jan-84
     SYSTEM.MISCINFO   1   2-Jan-84
     SYSTEM.FILER   39   31-Oct-84
     SYSTEM.LIBRARY   7   13-May-85
     SYSTEM.WRK.TEXT   4   26-Jul-85
     SYSTEM.WRK.CODE   2   26-Jul-85
     7/7 files <listed/in-dir>, 186 blocks used, 14 unused, 10 in largest

Make

Use
To create a disk file.

Prompt	Reply
Make what file?	file-spec size-spec

volume-name:file-name made

where *size-spec* is of the form [positive integer] or [0] or [*].

Notes
(1) *size-spec* is optional. If not present, the largest unused block on the disk will be allocated for the file. A *size-spec* of [0] will have the same effect while a *size-spec* of [*] will allocate the second largest unused area or half the largest

unused area, whichever is larger.
(2) A text file or code file will be allocated if the suffix .TEXT or .CODE appears in the file name.
(3) Text files must have an even number of blocks and must contain at least four.
(4) Wild cards may not appear in the *file-spec*.
(5) Make can sometimes be used to recover files accidentally removed from a directory. This is done by 'making' a file over the blocks on the disk containing the contents of the old file.

Examples
(1) Make what file? #5:NAMES[20]
    TEST:NAMES made
(2) Make what file? HANOI.TEXT[10]
    SYSTEM4:HANOI.TEXT made
(3) Make what file? EMPTY
    SYSTEM4:EMPTY made

New

Use
To clear the workfiles.

Save may be selected before New to keep a copy of existing workfiles. If there is an existing workfile when New is selected, the message

Throw away current workfile?

will appear, to which the answer 'y' or 'n' should be given. If the answer is 'y', the following message will be shown:

Workfile cleared

Example
Throw away current workfile? y
Workfile cleared

On/off-line

Use
To mount or dismount a subsidiary volume.

Prompt
Subsidiary Volume: M(ount, D(ismount, C(lear

If Mount is selected, the following appears:

Prompt	*Reply*
Mount what vol?	*file-spec*
volume-name:file-name —> Mounted	

where *file-spec* must specify a .SVOL file

Wild cards may be used in *file-spec* or several *file-specs* may appear separated by commas if a number of subsidiary volumes are to be mounted.

If Dismount is selected, the dialogue is:

Prompt	*Reply*
Dismount what vol?	*volume-id*
volume-name: —> Dismounted	

where *volume-id* specifies a subsidiary volume.

If Clear is selected, all subsidiary volumes which are mounted are dismounted.

Examples
(1) Mount what vol? #5:=
 mounts *all* subsidiary volumes on the disk referred to as #5

(2) Dismount what vol? #13:
    SUB: —> Dismounted

Prefix

Use
To specify a given volume as the default.

    Prompt   *Reply*
Prefix titles by what vol?   *volume-id*
Prefix is *volume-name:*

Notes
(1) The default volume can be referred to as : instead of the full *volume-id*.
(2) If the reply to the initial prompt is a *device number* corresponding to a disk drive containing a disk, then this disk becomes the default volume. If no disk is present, the drive itself is the default whatever volume may later be mounted on it.
(3) If the reply is a *volume-name* the volume need not be on-line at the time.
(4) The default volume is initially the volume from which the system was booted. A reply of * reinstates this volume as the default.

Example
Prefix titles by what vol? #5:
Prefix is TEST:

assuming the volume TEST is in #5.

Quit

Use
To leave the filer.

Remove

Use
To delete one or more files from a directory.

Prompt	*Reply*
Remove what file?	file-spec
volume-name:file-name —>removed	
Update directory?	y/n

Notes
(1) Remove should not be used to delete workfiles. New should be used instead.
(2) The third line gives you the chance to change your mind about deleting the file.
(3) Wild cards may be used in the *file-spec* (see example 2).

Examples
(1) Remove what file? :NAMES
    TEST:NAMES —> removed
    Update directory? y
(2) Remove what file? VERSION?
    Remove VERSION1.TEXT? y
    Remove VERSION2.TEXT? y
    Remove VERSION3.TEXT? n
    Update directory? y

Save

Use
To save copies of the TEXT and CODE workfiles.

If the workfiles were not set up using Get, since the system was initialized:

Prompt	Reply
Save as what file?	file-spec

Remove old *volume-name:file-name*.TEXT?   y/n   *
*syst-vol:*SYSTEM.WRK.TEXT —> *volume-name:file-name*.TEXT
Remove old *volume-name:file-name*CODE?   y/n   *
*syst-vol:*SYSTEM.WRK.CODE —> *volume-name:file-name*.CODE

* will appear if *file-spec* refers to an existing file.
syst-vol is the name of the SYSTEM disk.

Notes
(1) *file-spec* in line 1 should not include the suffix .TEXT or the suffix .CODE.
(2) If SYSTEM.WRK.TEXT or SYSTEM.WRK.CODE does not exist, then lines 2 to 4 or lines 5 to 7 will not appear. If neither file exists the message

    No workfile to save

    will appear.
(3) If the workfiles are saved on the system volume, the files SYSTEM.WRK.TEXT and SYSTEM.WRK.CODE will be renamed with the *file-name* specified. If the files are saved on another volume, SYSTEM.WRK.TEXT and

SYSTEM.WRK.CODE will remain on the system volume unaltered.
(4) Wild cards are not allowed.

If the workfiles were set up using Get, since the system was initialized:

Prompt	Reply
Save as *volume-name:file-name?*	y/n
Remove old *volume-name:file-name*.TEXT?	y/n

syst-vol:SYSTEM.WRK.TEXT —> *volume-name:file-name*.TEXT

Remove old *volume-name:file-name*.CODE? y/n

syst-vol:SYSTEM.WRK.CODE —> *volume-name:file-name*.CODE

Notes
(1) Answering 'n' to the first prompt leads to the previous dialogue. Answering 'n' to either of the other prompts leaves Save.
(2) If SYSTEM.WRK.TEXT or SYSTEM.WRK.CODE does not exist, then lines 2 to 4 or 5 to 7 will be missing.
(3) If the workfiles have not been altered since Get was selected, the message

    Workfile is saved

    will appear.
(4) Wild cards are not allowed.

Examples
(1) Save as what file? FOUR
    SYSTEM4:SYSTEM.WRK.TEXT —>
    TEST:FOUR.TEXT

```
        SYSTEM4:SYSTEM.WRK.CODE —>
        TEST:FOUR.CODE
(2)     Save as PASCAL:BINCHOP? y
        Remove old PASCAL:BINCHOP.TEXT? y
        SYSTEM4:SYSTEM.WRK.TEXT —>
        PASCAL:BINCHOP.TEXT
        Remove old PASCAL:BINCHOP.CODE? y
        SYSTEM4:SYSTEM.WRK.CODE —>
        PASCAL:BINCHOP.CODE
```

Transfer

Use
To copy a file or files; also to display or print files or to copy complete volumes.

To copy a file:

Prompt	*Reply*
Transfer what file?	*file-spec1*
To where?	*file-spec2*
Remove *volume-name2:file-name2*	y/n *

volume-name1:file-name1 —> *volume-name2:file-name2*

* appears if *file-spec2* already exists.

Notes
(1) To indicate that the copied file should have the same name as the original one, the reply to the 'To where' prompt could be

vol:$

where *vol* was the name of the destination volume.

(2) *file-spec2* could include a size specification in which case the file will be placed in the first unused portion of the disk which is at least as large as the size specification.

(3) By using wild cards, several files could be copied.

(4) The initial reply can specify the source *and* the destination files by typing

file-spec1, file-spec2

To display a file:

Prompt	Reply
Transfer what file?	*file-spec*
To where?	CONSOLE:

volume-name:file-name —> CONSOLE:

Notes

(1) #1 could have been used in place of CONSOLE:
(2) PRINTER: (or #6), in place of CONSOLE: would have listed the file on the printer.
(3) In order to enter a file from the keyboard, CONSOLE: (or #1) would have been given as the first reply and the name of a disk file as the second. The user would have to type <eof> to terminate the input.

To copy a complete volume:

Prompt	Reply
Transfer what file?	*volume-id1*

56

To where?	*volume-id2*
Transfer *m* blocks?	y/n
Blocks to transfer?	p *
Destroy *volume-name2*?	y/n **
volume-name1 —> *device-number2*	

m is the total number of blocks on the source volume.
p is a positive integer less than *m*
* appears if the previous reply is 'n'.
** appears if the destination volume has a valid directory.

Notes
(1) The two volumes should have *different* names.
(2) The two volumes should have the *same* capacity.

Examples
(1) Transfer what file? SYSTEM.EDITOR
    To where? PASCAL:SYSTEM.EDITOR
    SYSTEM4:SYSTEM.EDITOR —>
    PASCAL:SYSTEM.EDITOR
(2) Transfer what file? #4,#5
    Transfer 320 blocks? (Y/N) y
    SYSTEM4 —> #5
(3) Transfer what file? PROG?, PASCAL:$
    Transfer PROG.TEXT? y
    SYSTEM4:PROG.TEXT —>
    PASCAL:PROG.TEXT
    Transfer PROG.CODE? y
    SYSTEM4:PROG.CODE —>
    PASCAL:PROG.CODE

Volumes

Use
To display the names of the volumes which are on-line.

A typical response from this command would be:

Vols on-line
```
    1    CONSOLE:
    2    SYSTERM:
    4 #  SYSTEM4: [320]
    5 #  PASCAL: [320]
    7    REMIN:
    8    REMOUT:
   13 #  SUB:    [20] on volume SYSTEM4: stored at
block 104
```
Root vol is SYSTEM4:
Prefix vol is PASCAL:

Notes
(1) SYSTEM4: and PASCAL: are storage volumes (for storing files). SUB is a subsidiary volume on volume SYSTEM4. The other volumes are communication volumes (for input/output etc.). All the volumes listed (and no more) are accessible to the p-system.
(2) The Root vol is the volume used to boot the system. The prefix is the default volume.
(3) The figures in square brackets are the capacities of the disk volumes.

What

Use
To find out the names of the workfiles.

One of two responses will normally appear:

Workfile is *volume-name:file-name*

where the workfiles are permanent disk files;

Not named (not saved)

where temporary workfiles are being used, i.e.
SYSTEM.WRK.TEXT/CODE.

Notes
(1) If the workfiles are permanent disk files but the latest versions have not been saved, a message of the form

    Workfile is *volume-name:file-name*(not saved)

    will appear.
(2) If there is currently no workfile, the following message will appear:

    No workfile

Example
Workfile is PASCAL:SHELLSORT

eXamine

Use
To fix any bad blocks if possible.

Prompt	Reply
Examine blocks on what vol?	*volume-id*
Block range?	*range*
File(s) endangered	
file-name 1 *start finish*	
.	
.	
.	
Fix them?	y/n
Block *m* is bad	
Block *n* may be ok	
.	
.	
.	
Mark bad blocks?(Y/N)	y/n

range is of one of the forms

positive integer
positive integer – *positive integer*

and indicates the block or range of blocks to be examined. *start* and *finish* give the range of blocks occupied by a file.

Notes
(1) eXamine is usually used after Bad blocks has indicated that certain blocks are apparently bad. The files listed as being endangered are all those in the block range. A reply of 'n' to

Fix them?

will terminate eXamine. If, however, the reply is 'y', eXamine will attempt to check each block for physical damage by reading from it and

writing to it several times. Blocks which pass this test may be ok; blocks which do not pass the test are said to be bad.
(2) Bad blocks may be marked by replying 'y' to the last prompt. This is done by creating a file of type .BAD over them. Such a file will *not* be moved by Krunch.

Example
Examine blocks on what vol? PASCAL:
Block-range? 201
File(s) endangered:
PROG1.TEXT 200 250
Fix them? y
Block 201 is bad
Mark bad blocks? (Y/N) y

Zero

Use
To set up a new directory on a storage volume.

Prompt	Reply	
Zero dir of what vol?	volume-id	
Destroy *volume-name*?	y/n	*
Duplicate dir?	y/n	
Are there *m* blks on the disk?(Y/N)	y/n	*
# of blocks on the disk?	p	
New vol name?	volume-name:	
*volume-name:*correct?	y/n	
*volume-name:*zeroed		

where *p* is a positive integer. Lines marked * appear if the volume already has a directory. The second one gives the size of the volume and asks if the new directory is for a volume of the same size. If the volume does not have a directory already or you do not wish the volume to have the same number of blocks as previously, then you are asked to specify the number of blocks on the volume.

Notes
(1) The third prompt enquires whether a duplicate directory is required for security purposes.
(2) On most systems new disks must be formatted before being zeroed. The method by which disks are formatted is implementation dependent.

Example
Zero dir of what vol?:
Duplicate dir? n
# of blocks on the disk ? 320
New vol name? TEST:
TEST: correct? y
TEST: zeroed

The Editor

The editor is the system module for changing the contents of text files. The editor menu is

>Edit : A(djust C(opy D(el F(ind I(nsert J(ump K(ol M(argin P(age?[IV.1F7b]

the question mark indicating that further options can be obtained by typing '?'. These are:

>Edit:Q(uit R(plc S(et V(erify X(ch Z(ap [IV.1F7b]

Each of these commands is discussed in detail later in this section. First we introduce a few ideas.

Using the editor

The editor is screen orientated. The text currently being edited is held in the user's workspace, different parts of which can be viewed via the screen. The part of the workspace currently shown on the screen is known as the *window*. At the start of an editing session a file may be copied into the workspace and at the end of a session the contents of the workspace may be copied to a file. The cursor is used to indicate a particular character position in the window. Alterations to the workspace will normally take place at the cursor position.

The simplest method of moving the cursor is by means of the arrow keys which are normally used to implement the <up>, <down>, <left> and <right> special keys, the left and right arrow keys moving the cursor to the left and right respectively and the up and down arrow keys moving it up and down one character position at a time. It is not possible, however, to move the cursor outside the boundaries of the text itself. If, for example, the cursor is at the right-hand end of a line of text and the right arrow key is pressed, the cursor will be moved to the start of the next line of text. An integer, n say, typed before an arrow key is depressed will move the cursor n places in the appropriate direction; n is called the *repeat factor*. If '/' is used in place of a repeat factor, the cursor is moved 'as far as possible' in the required direction. Also on some computers, holding down the arrow key will cause repeated cursor movement in the direction appropriate to the arrow.

Other keys that can be used to move the cursor are

<space>, <bs>, <ret>, <tab>

which have the expected results as long as the direction indicator has not been altered. The direction indicator appears as the first character in the edit menu. By default it is '>' indicating forward motion through the text. Typing '<' changes the direction indicator to imply backwards motion, making the above four keys move the cursor in the opposite direction to what might have been expected. For example, depressing the tab key when the direction indicator is '<' will move the cursor to the previous tab position reading from left to right. The direction indicator can be reset by typing '>'. The effect of the arrow keys does not depend on the value of the direction indicator.

Repeat factors may be used with the four keys described above.

Other special keys used by the editor are <etx> (ctrl+c on the IBM PC) used to terminate insertions and deletions and <esc> used to leave a command.

eXchange also uses <exch-ins> and <exch-del>.

Literals and tokens

Some editor commands search for a particular string of text in a file. This can be done in literal or token mode. In literal mode any occurrence of the string may be identified. In token mode, however, only 'isolated' occurrences of the string will be identified, a string being deemed isolated if surrounded by spaces or other punctuation. Thus if the string being searched for is

write

in literal mode

writeln

may be identified whereas in token mode it will not. In addition token mode ignores spaces within strings so that

x := sin (a + b)

will be treated the same as

x:=sin(a+b)

Token mode is normally the default mode but this can be altered by using Set Environment.

Delimited strings

When a command requires a particular string to be specified, it normally has to be surrounded by two identical delimiters, acceptable delimiters being any available characters other than letters, digits or the space character, as long as the delimiter chosen does not appear elsewhere in the string. A string enclosed by delimiters is referred to as a *delimited string*. For example:

$write$
/end/
?begin?

are all examples of delimited strings and denote the strings

write
end
begin

respectively.

Copy buffer

A copy of the last piece of text which has been inserted or deleted is automatically kept in an area of memory called the copy buffer. Certain commands such as Copy can be used to place the contents of the copy buffer within the workspace being edited. By this means pieces of text can be moved from one part of the workspace to another or inserted in the workspace a number of times. Precise details of how to use the copy buffer are given in the descriptions of the following editor commands.

Adjust

Use
To move complete lines of text to the right or left or to centre them.

Prompt
>Adjust:L(just R(just C(enter <arrow keys>{<etx> to leave}

Notes
(1) Before selecting Adjust, the cursor will have been placed on the line to be adjusted.

 L will move the line as far left as possible
 R will move the line as far right as possible
 C will centre the line

(2) The left and right arrow keys can be used to move the line one character position to the left or right or more than one character position using repeat factors. After one line has been adjusted, the following (previous) line can be adjusted in the *same* way by pressing the down (up) arrow key. The 'current' adjustment is terminated by pressing <etx>.

(3) Text can be moved leftwards only as far as the left-hand edge of the screen. However, text can be moved rightwards until it disappears off the screen, though it is not lost and can be brought back into the window by moving it left again.

(4) The positions of the margins can be altered by means of Set Environment.

Copy

Use
To insert text from the copy buffer or from a text file.

Prompt   *Reply*
>Copy : B(uffer F(rom file <esc>

The B response will insert the complete text from the

copy buffer immediately before the current cursor position, the cursor being left in the character position immediately following the text inserted. The contents of the copy buffer may be inserted into the workspace in this way any number of times. The following commands insert text into the copy buffer:

Delete
Insert
Zap

In addition,

Margin

will leave the copy buffer empty.

The F response could lead to a dialogue of the following form:

>Copy: from what file[marker,marker]?   *file-spec*

where *file-spec* should not include .TEXT as this will be added automatically. The above reply will insert a complete file. To insert only part of a file, markers must have been inserted in the file, in which case a reply of the form

file-spec[*,marker*]

will insert text up to the *marker* named, while

file-spec[*marker,*]

will insert text from the *marker*, and

file-spec[*marker1,marker2*]

will insert the text between *marker1* and *marker2*. The use of markers is described in Set Marker.

Delete

Use
To remove a section of text from the workspace.

Prompt
>Delete:<><Moving commands>{<etx> to delete,<esc> to abort}

Notes
(1) Before selecting Delete, the cursor will have been positioned on the first character to be deleted. The cursor movement keys will then delete any text encountered by the cursor. Moving the cursor back towards the start of the deletion will restore the text.
(2) To accept a deletion, <etx> should be typed. <esc> can be used to abort.
(3) Repeat factors can be used with Delete and the direction indicator can be changed by typing '<' or '>'.
(4) Deleted text is copied into the copy buffer replacing its previous contents. Accidental deletions can therefore be 'undone' using Copy.
(5) If the text deleted will not fit in the copy buffer, the message

   There is no room to copy the deletion. Do you wish to delete anyway?

   will appear.

eXchange

See alphabetically under X

Find

Use
To locate a specified character string forwards or backwards from the cursor position.

Prompt	*Reply*
>Find[*n*]:L(it <target> =>	*delimited-string*

Notes
(1) *n* is a positive integer and will be 1 unless a repeat factor was entered before Find was selected. If, for example, a repeat factor of 3 was used, the third occurrence of the string would be located and 3 would appear in place of *n* in the prompt.
(2) Assuming token mode is the default, L should be typed before the *delimited-string* if a literal (rather than a token) is to be found. If, however, literal mode has been set as the default (by means of Set Environment), then T(ok will appear in the prompt menu in place of L(it. In this case T will have to be typed before the delimited string to find a token rather than a literal.
(3) If the string to be searched for is the same as in the last call of Find or Replace the user can type S rather than a *delimited string.*
(4) The direction of search will depend on the value of the direction indicator which may be altered prior to selecting Find.

Examples
(1) >Find[1]:L(it ,<target> => l/begin/
    will place the cursor after the first literal 'begin' after its present position.
(2) <Find[2]:L(it <target> => 'x/y'
    will place the cursor after the second token 'x/y' before the current position
(3) >Find[1]:L(it <target> => /write/
    will place the cursor after the first isolated 'write' after the current position.
(4) >Find[1]:L(it <target> => S
    (following the previous example) will place the cursor after the next isolated occurrence of 'write'.

Insert

Use
To insert new text into the (possibly empty) workspace.

Prompt
>Insert:Text{<bs> a char,<del> a line}[<etx> accepts, <esc> escapes]

Notes
(1) If a new file is being created, select Insert and begin typing the text to be inserted in the file. If a piece of text is being inserted into an existing file, first place the cursor over the character position immediately after the point where the insertion is to be made, then type the text to be inserted. In either case the insertion should be terminated with <etx>.

(2) While inserting text, <bs> can be used to delete the last character typed and <del> can be used to delete the current line. Space will be made on the screen to insert text as necessary.

(3) Typing <esc> during an insertion will abandon it.

(4) The format of the inserted text will to some extent depend on the values of the parameters set by Set Environment.

Jump

Use
To move the cursor to the beginning or the end of the workspace or to a marker.

Prompt
>Jump: B(eginning E(nd M(arker <esc>

The B and E options move the cursor to the beginning or the end of the workspace as appropriate. The M option generates the prompt

Jump to what marker?

the reply to which is the name of a marker in the file previously set by Set Marker.

Repeat factors are *not* allowed.

Example
>Jump: B(eginning E(nd M(arker <esc> M
Jump to what marker? Proc2

Kolumn

Use
To move text to the right or left; mainly useful in dealing with tables.

Prompt
>Kolumn:<vector keys>{<etx>,<esc> CURRENT line}

Notes
(1) Before selecting Kolumn the cursor will have been placed immediately to the left of the leftmost character position to be moved. After selecting Kolumn the right (or left) arrow key can be used to move all the text to the right of the cursor on the current line one character position to the right (or left). Repeat factors are not advised.
(2) Once Kolumn has been applied to a line of text, the corresponding change can be made to the following (or previous) line by pressing the down (or up) arrow key.
(3) As a result of using the left arrow key, text may be overwritten. This text *cannot* be recovered. Text moved off the screen to the right, however, *can* be recovered by moving it leftwards again.
(4) <esc> can be used within Kolumn to reinstate the current line only.

Margin

Use
To reformat the text in a paragraph to conform as closely as possible to the current environment.

Notes
(1) Before selecting Margin the cursor will have been placed somewhere within the paragraph to be reformatted.
(2) Margin will reformat the paragraph to conform as closely as possible with the current parameters set by Set Environment. Margin may not be used if Auto indent is true or Filling is false or the left- and right-hand margins do not have sensible values. In these cases the following message will appear:

Margin:Inappropriate environment. Please press <spacebar> to continue.

Page

Use
To display the next screenful of text.

Note
A repeat factor may be used and the direction indicator may have either value.

Quit

Use
To leave the editor.

For details of how Quit is used, see under command Edit of the main menu.

Replace

Use
To replace a given string by another one.

>   *Prompt*   *Reply*
> Replace[*n*]:L(it V(fy<targ><sub> => *d-s d-s*

where *d-s* is short for *delimited string*.

Notes
(1) The string to be replaced is called the *target string* (targ) and the string it is to be replaced by, the *substitution string* (sub). In the reply the first *delimited string* should be the target string and the second the substitution string. The same delimiter should be used in each case.
(2) *n* is a positive integer and will be 1 unless a repeat factor was entered before Replace was selected. If, for example, a repeat factor of 3 was used, this would mean that the next three occurrences of the target string were to be replaced.
(3) Assuming token mode is the default, L should be typed before the target string if a literal (rather than a token) is to be found. If, however, literal mode has been set as the default (by means of Set Environment), then T(ok will appear on the prompt menu in place of L(it. In this case T will have to be typed before the target string to find a token rather than a literal.

(4) If V is typed before the target string, the user will get the *option* of replacing each string matching the target up to a maximum of *n* times.

(5) The direction of search will depend on the value of the direction indicator which may be altered prior to selecting Replace.

Examples

(1) >Replace[1]:L(itV(fy <targ><sub>=>/
function//procedure/
will replace the next token 'function' by the token 'procedure' and leave the cursor immediately after the token 'procedure'.

(2) >Replace[2]:L(itV(fy <targ><sub>=>
L/read//write/
will replace the next two occurrences of the literal 'read' by the literal 'write' and leave the cursor immediately after the second substitution.

(3) >Replace[3]:L(it V(fy <targ><sub>=>
LV/write//writeln/
will move the cursor to the first occurrence of the literal write and the following prompt will be displayed:

Replace:<esc>aborts, 'R' replaces, ' ' doesn't

The R response will replace the occurrence indicated by the cursor whereas if the response is a space the replacement will not take place. The next two (i.e. a total of three) occurrences of the target string will be highlighted in the same way and the user given the opportunity of replacing each one with the substitution string.

However, the process will stop even if the limit given by the value of *n* has not been reached when there are no more occurrences of the target string to be considered. <esc> aborts at any stage.

Set

Use
To select Set Environment or Set Marker.

    Prompt
>Set:E(nvironment M(arker <esc>

Set Environment

Use
To display or alter the values of the formatting parameters.

    Prompt
>Environment:{Options} <spacebar> to leave
    A(uto indent   True
    F(illing   False
    L(eft margin   1
    R(ight margin   80
    P(ara margin   6
    C(ommand ch   ^
    S(et tabstops
    T(oken def   True

    n bytes used, *m* available

    Patterns:
<target>=*string*1, <subst>=*string*2

EDITING *file-spec*
Created *date1*; Last updated *date2*(revision *p*)
Editor version . . .

where *m, n* and *p* are positive integers and *date1* and *date2* are of the form

month day,year

The values shown for the options are the initial ones. Any option may be changed by typing its first letter followed by one of the following as appropriate:

T or *F*
a *positive integer* followed by return
a *character*

Line-oriented and paragraph-oriented editing
The editor can be tailored towards either line-oriented or paragraph-oriented editing by giving the options appropriate values. Line-oriented editing is more suitable for editing programs and certain types of data whereas paragraph-oriented editing is more suitable for editing text (like this Handbook for example). The meanings of the various parameters are now described.

Auto indent
When an insertion is being made, the effect of typing <ret> will depend on the value of Auto indent as follows:

Auto indent	*Effect*
true	Following line begins with the same indentation as the previous one

false	Following line begins at the left margin

The Margin command may only be selected when Auto indent is false.

Filling
Filling is usually false for line-oriented text and true for paragraph-oriented text with the following effects:

Filling	*Effect*
true	A return is automatically inserted when it is found that a word will not fit in the present line and the complete word is moved to the next line
	The Margin command is available
false	The user must insert his own returns
	Auto indent may be used
	The Margin command is not available

Left margin
The position of the left margin will normally be in column 1 of the screen but may be altered.

Right margin
The position of the right margin is in column 80 by default but is usually less in paragraph-oriented editing. Its value will affect the centring option in Adjust and the length of the lines if Filling is true.

Para margin
The first line of a paragraph may be indented (or outdented) relative to the rest of the text by typing

two consecutive <ret>s. The amount of the indentation will be the current value of Para margin (default 6 characters).

Command ch
The default value for Command ch is '^'. If this appears as the first non-blank character of a line, the line will not be affected by the Margin command selected when the cursor is positioned on a neighbouring line. On insertion, such a line will not be filled even if Filling is true. This facility is useful when the file being edited is to be input to a text formatter, in which case lines which contain formatting instructions can begin with Command ch. Many text formatters use '.' in place of '^'.

Set tabstops
Initially tabstops are in every eighth column but this can be altered. The S option leads to the following display:

Set tabs:<right, left vectors>C(ol # T(oggle tab <etx>
T-------T-------T-------T-------T-------T-------T-------
Column #1

indicating the default settings of the tabstops, T representing a column with a tabstop and - representing a column without a tabstop. The display would stretch to 80 columns. The cursor can be moved along this line using the arrow keys or by typing C followed by the column number in which the cursor is to be placed. To insert a new tabstop, position the cursor in the required column and type T.

Similarly to remove an existing tabstop, position the cursor in the required column and type T. When the tabstops have been set, <etx> will return to the Set Environment display.

Token def
This stands for token default. If it is true, token mode will be the default for the Find and Replace commands. If it is false, literal mode will be the default for these commands.

Word processing
For word processing and other paragraph-oriented applications the initial settings of the above parameters are not the most appropriate. In particular, Auto indent would normally be false and Filling would be true for such files. In addition, Right margin would be set to some appropriate value depending on the output medium.

Other information
Apart from the values of the various parameters, the Set Environment command gives certain other information which is largely self-explanatory. The most recent target and substitution strings used by the editor (if any) are given together with any markers present in the file (see Set Marker). The dates when the file was created and last updated are also shown.

Set Marker

Use
To place markers in the file being edited.

Prompt	*Reply*
Set what marker?	marker

Notes
(1) Before selecting Set Marker the cursor will have been positioned at the point in the workspace where the marker is to be placed. The reply to the prompt will be the name of the marker. This will consist of up to eight alphanumeric characters, upper- and lower-case letters being considered distinct.
(2) Up to 20 markers may be inserted in a file.
(3) If an attempt is made to set a twenty-first marker, a display such as the following will appear:

Marker ovflw. Which one to replace? (Type in the letter or <sp>)

a)marker1	b)marker2	c)marker3
d)marker4	e)marker5	f)marker6
g)marker7	h)marker8	i)marker9
j)marker10	k)marker11	l)marker12
m)marker13	n)marker14	o)marker15
p)marker16	q)marker17	r)marker18
s)marker19	t)marker20	

(4) Markers are used in conjunction with the Jump and Copy commands.

Verify

Use
To re-display the current window.

This command is occasionally useful to check that the text on the screen actually corresponds to what is in the workspace. Repeat factors are not allowed.

eXchange

Use
To alter the workspace by overwriting existing text.

Prompt
>eXchange:Text <vector keys> {<etx>,<esc> CURRENT line}

Notes
(1) After selecting eXchange the cursor may be moved around the screen using any of the cursor movement keys *except* space. Typing text (including spaces) will overwrite whatever characters were previously present. At any instant the cursor will show the character about to be overwritten.
(2) Space may be made for an extra character or a character may be deleted by depressing the <exch-ins> key or the <exch-del> key as appropriate.
(3) Typing <etx> will accept the changes made. <esc> will exit from eXchange undoing the changes to the *current* line only.
(4) eXchange ignores the value of the direction indicator.
(5) Repeat factors are *not* allowed.

Zap

Use
To delete text between the first character of the string most recently found, replaced or inserted and the present cursor position.

Notes
(1) Typing = will place the cursor over the first character of the string most recently found, replaced or inserted if this is not known.
(2) If an attempt is made to Zap more than 80 characters, the prompt appears:

WARNING :You are about to Zap more than 80 chars,do you wish to Zap?(y/n)

(3) The text removed by Zap will be kept in the copy buffer. If there is not sufficient room the user will be warned.
(4) Zap may not be selected after Adjust, Delete, Kolumn or Margin.

Utilities

A number of utility programs are available in the UCSD system. Some are machine specific and are not discussed here. Others perform machine-independent functions and are in some ways similar to commands but, because of their relatively infrequent use, are not accessed via the main menu but by selecting the command eXecute and replying to the prompt.

Execute what file?

with a *file-spec* including the name of the utility.

Many of the utilities are extremely versatile and only their more common uses are described.

MARKDUPDIR

Use
To create a duplicate directory on a disk which does not have one.

When the filer option Extended list is selected, the directory of a disk will show files (or unused portions) starting at block 6 if no duplicate directory is held and at block 10 if one is held. MARKDUPDIR will create a duplicate directory in blocks 6 to 9 of a disk. These blocks must therefore be free for use before MARKDUPDIR is executed. Extended list can be used to check this and files can be moved if necessary. The filer option Krunch with block 6 as the starting block will move the files away from blocks 6 to 9 as long as there is sufficient space at the other end of the disk.

The dialogue for MARKDUPDIR is something like the following:

| *Prompt* | *Reply* |

Duplicate Directory Marker{July 13,1978}
Enter drive# of user's disk[4 or 5]: *4/5*
A duplicate directory is not being maintained on *volume-name:*
WARNING! It appears that blocks 6–9 are not free for use
Are you sure they are free? *y/n*
Do you want the directories to be marked *y/n*
Directories are now marked as duplicate. Type <ret> to exit.

COPYDUPDIR

Use
To copy a duplicate directory into the main directory.

If the main directory has become corrupt for any reason, COPYDUPDIR may be used to reinstate it provided a duplicate directory is being held.

The dialogue for COPYDUPDIR is something like the following:

Prompt	Reply
Duplicate Directory Copier{July 12,1978}	
Enter drive# of user's disk[4 or 5]:	4/5
Are you sure you want to zap directory of *volume-name*:{blocks 2–5}?	y/n
Directory copy is complete. Type <ret> to exit.	

RECOVER

Use
To recover lost files.

RECOVER attempts to reinstate files which have been removed from a disk's directory for some reason.

The dialogue for RECOVER is something like the following:

Prompt	Reply
Recover[1V.1H]	
USER'S DISK IN DRIVE # (0 exits)	*device-number*
USER'S VOLUME-ID	*volume-name*
How many blocks on disk?	*m*

where *m* is a positive integer.

A list of all the files currently in the directory then appears, followed by:

Are there still IMPORTANT files missing?(Y/N)	y/n

87

A reply of 'n' leads to

GO AHEAD AND UPDATE
DIRECTORY?(Y/N)   y/n

whereas a reply of 'y' causes RECOVER to search the complete disk for text and code files (recognizable by their format) which are not currently in the directory. Data files cannot be recognized in this way.

If the names of any such text and code files are not available, RECOVER will give each one a name of the form

DUMMY12X.TEXT

or with the .CODE suffix as appropriate. If the name of such a file is available and clashes with a file name already in the directory, two unique digits are added to the name. For each file that RECOVER is able to identify, a line of the following form will appear:

file DUMMY12X.TEXT inserted at blocks #m-p

where m and p are positive integers ($m < p$). Finally, the prompt

GO AHEAD AND UPDATE DIRECTORY(Y/N)?   y/n

appears, to which 'y' should be replied if you are happy with the reconstruction job which RECOVER has just done.

SETUP

Use
To alter the values of certain implementation or terminal-dependent constants.

The file SYSTEM.MISCINFO contains a list of constants which are read in when the system is initialized. These constants are parameters of the implementation and mostly depend on the type of terminal being used. Their values can be changed using SETUP. A full list of the constants involved is given in the Appendix.

The dialogue for SETUP is something like the following:

Prompt
INITIALIZING........................
....
SETUP: C(HANGE T(EACH H(ELP Q(UIT [D6]

The normal reply is to select CHANGE giving:

CHANGE: S(INGLE) P(ROMPTED) R(ADIX)
       L(IST) H(ELP) Q(UIT)

the usual reply being to select PROMPTED giving:

FIELD NAME = BACKSPACE
  OCTAL DECIMAL HEXADECIMAL
    302   194   C2
WANT TO CHANGE THIS VALUE?(Y,N,!)

A reply of 'Y' will lead to

NEW VALUE:

the reply to which is to press the key to be used for <backspace> which will lead to something like:

```
OCTAL DECIMAL HEXADECIMAL
 300      192      C0
```
WANT TO CHANGE THIS VALUE?(Y,N,!)

'N' will lead to

FIELD NAME = CODE POOL BASE[FIRST WORD]
```
OCTAL DECIMAL HEXADECIMAL
  0       0        0
```
WANT TO CHANGE THIS VALUE?(Y,N,!)

A reply of 'N' will lead to a similar display for the next option and so on. If no more options are to be changed, you should reply with '!' which will produce

CHANGE: S(INGLE) P(ROMPTED) R(ADIX)
    L(IST) H(ELP) Q(UIT)

QUIT leads to

SETUP: C(HANGE T(EACH H(ELP Q(UIT [D6]

Selecting QUIT again gives

QUIT: D(ISK) OR M(EMORY) U(PDATE),
       R(ETURN) H (ELP) E(XIT)

D will create an updated version of SYSTEM.MISCINFO called NEW.MISCINFO on the system disk.
M will update some of the constants in the memory.
R will return to the last section of dialogue.
H will produce HELP information.
E will EXIT from SETUP.

If D or M is chosen,

QUIT: D(ISK) OR M(EMORY) U(PDATE)
       R(ETURN) H(ELP) E(XIT)

will again appear. This time, EXIT should be chosen.

If NEW.MISCINFO is created it should be copied into SYSTEM.MISCINFO before the system is re-initialized if the new values are to be used. SYSTEM.MISCINFO should probably be backed up first.

QUICKSTART

Use
To make a program start quicker.

The QUICKSTART utility is used to set up tables describing a program's environment and to store them in the code file to save them having to be set up each time the program is run. It is useful when a program consists of many units.

The dialogue for QUICKSTART is something like the following:

    Prompt
Quickstart: P(rogram, S(ystem, C(opy, L(ibrary, M(essages, Q(uit

Toggle settings: Copy OFF, Library copy OFF, Messages OFF

The toggle options may each be ON or OFF. Selecting Copy, Library or Messages will change the state of the corresponding toggle option.

The normal response to the above prompt, apart from altering the toggle options, is to select Program causing the following prompt:

Quickstart what program?   *file-spec*

the .CODE suffix being added automatically to *file-spec*.
If Copy is ON the prompt

To what code file?

will appear. A possible answer is

volume-id $

meaning a file with the same name as the original file supplied to QUICKSTART but on some other disk. Alternatively, a *file-spec* to which the suffix .CODE may be added will do. If Message is ON you will get a listing of the compilation units being copied and various other information. If Copy is OFF the original code file is modified. Library copy is normally left OFF.

Eventually the message

Quickstart construction complete

will appear.

The System option is intended for Quickstarting system programs such as SYSTEM.PASCAL.

XREF

Use

To give information concerning the static or dynamic structure of a program and/or give tables of variables and the routines that can access them.

XREF is, among other things, a cross-referencing tool and is used to assist in the interpretation of (large) Pascal programs. It can be used in a number of ways and the dialogue goes something like the following:

Prompt	*Reply*
PROCEDURAL CROSS-REFERENCER VERSION S.02-IV.0.b	
How wide is your output device? [40...132]	80
Please enter the file you wish Cross-Referenced	file-spec
Is this a compiled listing?[y/n]	y/n
Do you want intrinsics listed?[y/n]	y/n
Do you want initial procedure nestings? [y/n]	y/n
Do you want procedure called by trees? [y/n]	y/n
Do you want variables referenced?[y/n]	y/n
Do you want variable called by trees:? [y/n]	y/n
Do you wish warnings?[y/n]	y/n
Please enter your warning file name:	file-spec
Please enter your output file name:	file-spec

Notes
(1) The .TEXT suffix should appear in *file-spec* where appropriate.
(2) Intrinsics correspond to standard functions and procedures in Pascal.
(3) 'initial procedure nestings' gives a list of all the procedures in a program and the procedures that each procedure calls.
(4) 'procedure called by trees' gives a list of all the procedures in a program and all the procedures that call each procedure.
(5) If variables are to be 'referenced', an alphabetical list of all the procedures in a program is produced showing all the variables, local or otherwise, which each procedure accesses. This is known as the variable reference table.
(6) 'variable call by trees' gives the name of all procedures that access each variable.
(7) If the variable reference table is produced, a warnings file may also be output. There are three types of warnings which may appear in the file:

symbol may be undeclared line #*mmm*
symbol may not be initialized line #*mmm*
not standard, nested comments line #*mmm*

where *mmm* is some integer value. The last type of warning refers to the fact that comments may not be nested in ISO standard Pascal, though they may in UCSD Pascal.

The behaviour of XREF when presented with a Pascal program containing syntax errors is not guaranteed.

LIBRARY

Use
To put separately compiled units or programs into a single file.

The LIBRARY utility is used to copy compiled units (or programs) from one or more input files to an output file. After

Library[z12]

has appeared at the top of the screen, the prompt

Output file?

appears halfway down the screen. The reply should be a suitable *file-spec* which must end in .CODE. The next prompt is

Input file?

near the top of the screen. The reply is a suitable *file-spec* to which .CODE will be added automatically. LIBRARY will then list all the units etc. in the file giving their slot number (position in the file), type, name and length, for example:

0   u   TRIG   404

where 'u' stands for 'unit'. Finally the LIBRARY menu appears at the very top of the screen:

Library:N(ew,0-9(slot to slot,E(very,S(elect, C(omp-unit,F(ill?[z12]

Some of the options available are:

N   to choose a new input file

E	to copy every unit etc. from the input file to the output file
0–9	to copy a 'unit' from a slot in the input file to a slot in the output file
S	for prompted copying
C	for copying by name
F	to copy all the compilation units referred to by segment references in the output file
A	to quit LIBRARY without copying to the output file

There are several other options used less frequently.

DECODE

Use
To access information held in code files.

The DECODER utility can be used to obtain symbolic listings of code segments held in code files and also the text of the interface sections of units. The dialogue for DECODE is something like the following:

Prompt	*Reply*
UCSD Code File Decoder IV.0[c.1]	
input file[<CR> to quit]:	*file-spec*

The .CODE suffix should *not* be included in *file-spec*.

Listing file[CONSOLE:]:   *file-spec*

CONSOLE: is the default indicated by <ret>.

Segment Guide: A(11),#(dct index),D(ictionary, Q(uit)

A	gives a symbolic listing of all segments in the file
D	lists the segment dictionary for the code file
Q	quits DECODE
#	where # is a positive integer, is used to obtain a symbolic listing of one or all of the procedures in segment #, the value of # being obtained from the segment dictionary.

Selecting # leads to something like:

There are 3 procedures in segment COMPLIST
Procedure Guide: A(ll),#(of Procedure), L(inker info),C(onstant pool),S(egment references), I(nterface text),Q(uit)

A	gives a symbolic listing of the complete segment
#	gives a symbolic listing of procedure #

and so on.

Apart from the initial display, the DECODE menu appears at the foot of the screen.

PRINT

Use
To print text files.

The utility PRINT can be used to paginate text and to control the vertical layout of text on a page. The menu for PRINT fills the complete screen.

Print[]:Select an option (type "?" for help):

> I(nput —>
> O(utput —> PRINTER:
> G(o. Print the Input file on the output
> A(dvance. Skip to the next page of the output
> M(ake script file for setting current parameters
> Q(uit. Leave this program

No	D(ouble space the lines?
No	N(umber the lines?
No	S(top before each page for single sheet loading?
Yes	U(se ASCII formfeed characters between pages?
1	F(irst page number
1	T(op margin size in lines
3	B(ottom margin size in lines
66	P(age size in lines (total: includes margins and heading)
\	E(scape sequence start-character
.	C(ommand line start-character
	H(eader —> Page \page. File is "\file". Printed on \date.

The values on the extreme left of the menu are the default ones.

In simple cases, a text file can be printed by executing the following steps:

(1) select the Input option and supply a *file-spec*,

(2) select the Go option,
(3) select the Quit option.

Other options are also available, for example:

Double space	to produce double-spaced text
Page length	to specify the number of lines per page (if other than 66)
Top	to specify the size of the top margin, i.e. number of lines of print
Bottom	to specify the size of the bottom margin

In addition, commands can be placed within the text in the text file which will affect its layout when it is PRINTed. For example, if a line begins with the command character (normally '.'), then it is not regarded as part of the text to be printed. The first two characters after the command character may stand for a PRINT command which will be executed when PRINT encounters it. Some of the commands available are:

COMMAND	followed by a single character in quotes, to change the command character to the character given
END	to indicate end of file
ESCAPE	followed by a single character in quotes, to change the escape character to the character given
HEADING	followed by a string in double quotes, to supply a heading for each page
INCLUDE	followed by a *file-spec*, to start processing *file-spec* in place of the

	current file returning to the current file when *file-spec* has been completely processed
PAGE	to take a new page on the output device

Another way by which commands may be placed within a file is by using the escape character, which may be followed by

PAGE
FILE
DATE

the effect of which will be to insert the current page number, file name or date in place of the escape sequence in the text.

Examples of command lines are:

.HEADING "UCSD Guide\PAGE"
.PAGE
.COMMAND '?'

There are several other options available with PRINT which are not described here. The utility SPOOLER can also be used to allow files to be printed in parallel with other activities.

COMPRESSOR

Use
To transform code files into a form in which they can be run outside the P-system environment.

Appendix

Fields of SETUP

BACKSPACE
CODE POOL BASE[FIRST WORD]
CODE POOL BASE[SECOND WORD]
CODE POOL SIZE
EDITOR ACCEPT KEY
EDITOR ESCAPE KEY
EDITOR EXCHANGE-DELETE KEY
EDITOR EXCHANGE-INSERT KEY
ERASE LINE
ERASE SCREEN
ERASE TO END OF LINE
ERASE TO END OF SCREEN
FIRST SUBSIDIARY VOL NUMBER
HAS 8510A
HAS BYTE FLIPPED MACHINE
HAS CLOCK
HAS EXTENDED MEMORY
HAS LOWER CASE
HAS RANDOM CURSOR ADDRESSING
HAS SLOW TERMINAL
HAS SPOOLING
HAS WORD ORIENTED MACHINE
KEYBOARD INPUT MASK
KEY FOR BREAK
KEY FOR FLUSH
KEY FOR STOP
KEY TO ALPHA LOCK
KEY TO DELETE CHARACTER
KEY TO DELETE LINE

KEY TO END FILE
KEY TO MOVE CURSOR DOWN
KEY TO MOVE CURSOR LEFT
KEY TO MOVE CURSOR RIGHT
KEY TO MOVE CURSOR UP
LEAD IN FROM KEYBOARD
LEAD IN TO SCREEN
MAX NUMBER OF SUBSIDIARY VOLS
MAX NUMBER OF USER SERIAL VOLS
MOVE CURSOR HOME
MOVE CURSOR RIGHT
MOVE CURSOR UP
NONPRINTING CHARACTER
PREFIXED[DELETE CHARACTER]
PREFIXED[EDITOR ACCEPT KEY]
PREFIXED[EDITOR ESCAPE KEY]
PREFIXED[EDITOR EXCHANGE-DELETE KEY]
PREFIXED[EDITOR EXCHANGE-INSERT KEY]
PREFIXED[ERASE LINE]
PREFIXED[ERASE SCREEN]
PREFIXED[ERASE TO END OF LINE]
PREFIXED[ERASE TO END OF SCREEN]
PREFIXED[KEY TO DELETE CHARACTER]
PREFIXED[KEY TO DELETE LINE]
PREFIXED[KEY TO MOVE CURSOR DOWN]
PREFIXED[KEY TO MOVE CURSOR LEFT]
PREFIXED[KEY TO MOVE CURSOR RIGHT]
PREFIXED[KEY TO MOVE CURSOR UP]
PREFIXED[MOVE CURSOR HOME]
PREFIXED[MOVE CURSOR RIGHT]
PREFIXED[MOVE CURSOR UP]
PREFIXED[NONPRINTING CHARACTER]
PRINTABLE CHARACTERS

SCREEN HEIGHT
SCREEN WIDTH
SEGMENT ALIGNMENT
STUDENT
VERTICAL MOVE DELAY

Index

How to use this Handbook 1

Adjust 5,22,63,66,84
Ammann, Urs 2
Assemble 3,5,12
Auto indent 74,77,78,79,81
Bad blocks 5,32,33,37,38, 46,59,60
Bowles, Professor Kenneth 2
break points 21
Change 5,25,32,36,39
Command 3,4
Command ch 77,80
command file 27,28
Command line start-character 98
communications volume 33,58
Compile 3,5,9,10,11,14
compiler option 11,18
COMPRESSOR 100
conditional compilation 20
CONSOLE 34,58
Copy 5,22,63,66,67,69,82
copy buffer 10,66,67,68,69, 84
COPYDUPDIR 86
COPYRIGHT 19
Date 5,25,32,40
Debug 3,5,21
DECLARE 19,20,21
DECODE 96
default prefix 29,30
default volume 13,15,33,34, 51,58
Delete 5,22,63,68,69,84
delimited string 65,66,70,75
device number 33,51
direction indicator 64,69,70, 74,76,83
directory 37,41,42,46,47,52, 61,62,85,87
duplicate directory 37,62, 85,86
Edit 3,5,6,9,21,75
edit menu 63,64
Editor 1,63
Eidgenossische Technische Hochschule 2

Escape sequence start-character 98
eXamine 5,41,59
eXchange 5,69
eXecute 3,5,10,28,85
Execution option 28
Ext-dir 32,41
Extended list 5,36,41,42,46,85
File 3,5,6,25
file-spec 12,35,36
file types 36
Filling 74,77,79,80,81
Filer 1,4,32
filer menu 25,32
Find 5,22,63,70,81
Flip-swap/lock 5,32,43
Get 5,25,32,44,53,54
Halt 4,5,25,31
IBM PC 2,7,64
I/O CHECK 19
INCLUDE 19
Initialize 4,5,26,31
Insert 5,22,63,68,71
intrinsics 93,94
Jump 5,22,63,72,82
Keyboard 3,6,34
Kolumn 5,22,63,73,84
Krunch 5,32,45,46,61,86
Ldir 25,32
Left margin 77,79
LIBRARY 95
LIBRARY utility 12
Ljust 67
Link 3,5,12,26
LIST 19
List directory 5,36,46
literal mode 65,70,75,81
literals 65,70,75
Make 5,32,35,37,48
main menu 4,12,23,25,31,75,85
manufacturer's logo 4
Margin 5,22,63,68,74,79,80,84
MARKDUPDIR 85
Marker 5,68,72
memlocked 44
memswapped 44
Menus 4

Monitor 4,5
New 5,25,32,49,52
On-off-line 5,32,36,37,50
P-code 2,21
PAGE 20
Para margin 77,79,80
Pascal systems 2,10
Prefix vol 5,32,51,58
PRINTER 34
Pseudo-code 2
QUICKSTART 91
QUIET 20
Quit 4,5,22,23,24,25,32,52, 63,74
RANGE CHECK 20
RECOVER 87,88
REMIN 34,58
REMOUT 34,58
Remove 5,25,32,36,52
repeat factor 64,67,69,70, 72,73,74,75,83
Replace 5,63,70,75,76,81
Right margin 77,79,81
Rjust 67
Root vol 58
Run 3,5,9,28
Save 5,25,32,44,49,52
scratch input buffer 10,30,31
separate compilation 11
Serial input 34
Serial output 34
Set 5,63,77
Set Environment 65,67,70, 72,74,75,77,81
Set Marker 68,72,77,81
Set tabstops 77,80
SETUP 89
size specification 35,48,56
special keys 2,6,63
SPOOLER 100
stack options 18,21
starting up 3
storage volume 33,37,58,61

subsidiary volume 33,37,46,50, 58
substitution string 75,76
symbolic listings 96,97
SYSTEM.ASSMBLER 14
SYSTEM.FILER 46
SYSTEM.LINKER 26
SYSTEM.LST.TEXT 10,19
SYSTEM.MISCINFO 89,91
SYSTEM.PASCAL 46
SYSTEM.WRK.CODE 13,14,15, 44,53,54,59
SYSTEM.WRK.TEXT 12,13,14, 23,44,53,54,59
SYSTERM 34,58
target string 75,76
Token def 77,81
token mode 65,70,75,81
Transfer 5,25,32,36,55
UCSD Pascal 2,11,94
units 11,95
University of California at San Diego 2
User restart 4,5,28
USES 20
Utilities 1,85
Verify 5,63,82
volume-id 33,34
volume-name 33,34
Volumes 5,37,59
warnings 93,94
What 5,25,32,58
wild cards 35,36,39,42,44,47, 49,50,52,54,56
window 63
workfiles 9,10,12,13,14,22,24, 28,44,49,53,54,59
workspace 10,22,23,24,63,66, 68,69,71,72,82,83
Xecute 3,5
XREF 93
Zap 5,63,68,84
Zero 5,32,61

Computer Handbooks

Languages

Assembly Language for the 80286   Robert Erskine
Assembly Language for the 8086 and 8088   Robert Erskine
C Language   Friedman Wagner-Dobler

Business Applications

dBASE III   Peter Gosling
Lotus 1–2–3   Dick Waller
SuperCalc and SuperCalc2   Peter Gosling
VisiCalc   Peter Gosling

Microcomputers

The Amstrad 464 and 664   Boris Allan
The Apricot   Peter Gosling
The Sinclair QL   Guy Langdon and David Heckingbottom

Operating Systems

Introduction to Operating Systems   Lawrence Blackburn and Marcus Taylor
The UCSD p-system   Robin Hunter

Word Processing

WordStar   Maddie Labinger and Jan Osborne
WordStar 2000   David Hawgood
Wordwise and Wordwise+   Wendy Chuter

Pocket Guides

Programming

Programming   John Shelley
Statistical Programming   Boris Allan
BASIC   Roger Hunt
COBOL   Ray Welland
FORTH   Steven Vickers
FORTRAN   Philip Ridler
FORTRAN 77   Clive Page
LOGO   Boris Allan
Pascal   David Watt

Assembly Languages

Assembly Language for the 6502   Bob Bright
Assembly Language for the 8085   Noel Morris
Assembly Language for the MC 68000 Series   Robert Erskine
Assembly Language for the Z80   Julian Ullmann

Microcomputers

Acorn Electron   Neil Cryer and Pat Cryer
Commodore 64   Boris Allan
Programming for the Apple   John Gray
Programming for the BBC Micro   Neil Cryer and Pat Cryer
Sinclair Spectrum   Steven Vickers
The IBM PC   Peter Gosling

Operating Systems

CP/M   Lawrence Blackburn and Marcus Taylor
MS-DOS   Val King and Dick Waller
PC-DOS   Val King and Dick Waller
UNIX   Lawrence Blackburn and Marcus Taylor

Word Processors

Introduction to Word Processing   Maddie Labinger
IBM Displaywriter   Jacquelyne A. Morison
Philips P5020   Peter Flewitt
Wang System 5   Maddie Labinger